HOUSE RULES

HOUSE RULES

AN ARCHITECT'S GUIDE TO MODERN LIFE

Deborah Berke

Essay by Rick Moody

Afterword by Marc Leff

Edited by Tal Schori

with Anne Thompson and Matthew Zuckerman

RIZZOLI
NEW YORK

First published in the United States of America in 2016 by
Rizzoli International Publications, Inc.
300 Park Avenue South
New York, NY 10010
www.rizzoliusa.com

ISBN: 978-0-8478-4821-8
LCCN: 2015957387

Designed by Miko McGinty and Anjali Pala

Printed and bound in China

2016 2017 2018 2019 2020 / 10 9 8 7 6 5 4 3 2 1

CONTENTS

Introduction

DEBORAH BERKE

A house is the most universal of structures. In its essence, it accommodates primal activities common to how all people live. We eat, sleep, bathe, do things in solitude, and do things in groups. That's it. That's the whole thing. These commonalities transcend cultural norms as well as other determining factors such as nationality, ethnicity, social class, and financial status. The elements of how people live operate at a basic level that has been there since the beginning of civilization: it tracks from the igloo to the castle. Individual houses might look different, but all houses are alike in having to satisfy the same set of core requirements.

None of those requirements comes with a predetermined aesthetic. The beauty of the house lies in its style neutrality. A house accommodates the functions of daily life and the pleasures of human existence. Nothing about that description prescribes elements like a flat roof, a paneled library, or a three-car garage. These are choices that reflect conceptions of "home"—a word quite different from "house." Home is adjectival and personal, something that conjures a wide range of associations determined by history, culture, and taste. "House"—in its noun-ness—is a place and a thing and carries no such limitations. This linguistic distinction is very important. A house presents an open condition in which the architect creates buildings consistent in facilitating basic human needs yet unique in reflecting the infinitely various combinations of geographic location and individual desire.

Needs and desires intersect around solitude and togetherness. We want and need to spend time alone and with others. A house must provide spaces for both conditions to happen with ease and in comfort. People do all kinds of things collectively. Making music, telling stories, and preparing food are just a few examples. Eating together is one of the great things that human beings do, in extravagance or simplicity, as celebration or routine. A shared meal can be as organized as Thanksgiving with turkey and dressing served on fine china in the dining room, or as casual as a bowl of cereal while reading the newspaper at the kitchen counter. People also spend time in groups doing a variety of different things individually, such as reading, checking e-mail, listening to music, or playing video games. This "alone but together" experience often happens when we are most relaxed with the people around us. The organic flow of the house should accommodate all modes of togetherness.

I decided to become an architect at age fourteen. On summer nights, I would stroll around my neighborhood, the place I grew up, with a friend who was a few years older and had already chosen architecture as his career. While walking, we would look at the houses, which were close together but each distinct. Based on what we could see and hear from the street—lights and colors, often filtered through closed drapes, and sounds drifting from open doors and windows—we would try to determine which rooms served which purposes and what people were doing in them. The narrative of what actually went on inside each house, of course, remained mysterious. But just from the exterior, regardless of a house's style or time period, we could always glean some sense of a story. We understood, without being able to articulate it precisely, that some rooms had highly specific functions while others were gathering places for a range of activities.

After I became an architect, that early sense of curiosity about the house and its uses seemed prescient when I started to question the number and kind of rooms that are necessary. What spaces do people really need for basic human tasks, duties, and pleasures? What became clear to me was that designers, and we as a culture, should move away from "destination rooms"—places where specific activities happen in isolation—to spaces that allow people to encounter each other and that invite conversation or group activities. Houses could be more direct, less unnecessarily complicated, and possibly smaller. A single house might have a library, a den, a family room, and a parlor, but these are all rooms that are, essentially, about doing the same thing. Too many rooms for the same purpose atomize rather than collect activity. It is better for rooms to serve multiple functions, i.e., a dining room lined with shelves of books, where people read or play cards at the table as well as eat meals. Even when people are not spending time in the same room, a house can facilitate feelings of connection. Rooms located within paths of circulation connect occupants as they move around. Rooms connected to each other by sightlines allow people not only to glimpse or observe each other, but also to experience a house from different vantage points. A slight shift in floor level, such as a sunken living room, can enclose spaces for privacy or conversation or orient perspectives outward, aligning eye level with corridors or windows. Rooms can appear differently or be appreciated anew depending on how and when they are used and the range of their potential uses. A room that on occasion can hold a dozen people for cocktails or dinner can also, in a more regular way, be a place where an individual can feel equally good spending time alone.

I believe opportunities for respite are essential. With the increasing presence of technology, the idea of having a space where we can be alone—where we can disconnect—is even more significant. Sometimes we burden alone time with the expectation that we will accomplish something profound or long overdue. We attach a kind of magic to solitude that depends on environment. We believe we can start a novel, meditate, or take time to relax only once we have the perfect space. But the fact is that alone time—and the space to facilitate it—can happen anywhere. The simple relationship of a chair to a window or the position of a fireplace or a folding screen can provide privacy. The goal of a house, then, is to make sure it contains a versatile kind of comfort, with spaces that encourage community but also provide the security that allows for solitude.

Given the essential neutrality of the house—and the core functions it serves—I have always felt that the architect operates as a "distiller" and a "tailor." Although both terms refer to processes of making something from scratch within parameters, they connote different actions: a tailor accommodates existing conditions, while the distiller combines, refines, and reduces to extract the purest and finest results. Architects do all these things, often simultaneously. They take the concept of "house" and define its character based on external pressures and conditions. One set of parameters comes from the property, in its qualities (usually profound) and restrictions (usually legal, such as zoning and building codes). Another set comes from the clients, in their habits and preferences. Some requirements are shared by many people, such as the need for morning light in the kitchen. Others are more specific: a couple with six children and fifteen grandchildren wants a space where everyone can sit at the same table

twice a year. Requests can be small but still definite and important: the left-handed person prefers the dishwasher to the left of the sink. And many of the things people want are intangible: a person who loves the sound of a foghorn longs for windows that open on the bay. Such wishes often go unstated but can be intuited in how a client talks. Here, the architect senses and provides opportunities for people to experience poetry in their daily lives. A site, too, can carry poetic potential in its orientation and materials. Walls built from stone discovered while excavating space for a basement literally ground a house in its property, beautifully blurring the built and the natural environment in a way no one could have articulated in advance.

Within every property, there are things the architect can and cannot change, or, to continue the metaphor, tailor. Each landscape or place has *terroir*, a rooted, essential quality that contains its history. Legal stipulations such as property lines, rights of way, height restrictions, and historical zoning must be obeyed. Yet the physical landscape can be altered or resisted to maximize its unique character or suit the wishes of the occupant. With an open field, perhaps plant more trees or orient the view toward an expansive meadow. You work with what is good and change what is not. If a house is in a dense city or neighborhood, surrounded by other buildings, you can embrace the prevailing aesthetic or reject it absolutely. If the houses on a street all look the same, a new building can assert independence, an intention to stand out and be pointedly other. Perhaps the front door is hidden on the side or the cladding is metal instead of wood. If zoning includes height limitations, the initial instinct might be to build to the maximum allowed. The shrewd architect will resist that impulse unless it serves the purpose of securing an amazing view or privacy. It might be more advantageous to stay low to the ground. No decision is automatic.

A long list of desires and requirements activates the role of distiller. The architect works to avoid excess and redundancy, not to be frugal but to be inventive, to make houses with active spaces that celebrate nonwasteful expansiveness. Obviously, where you bathe does not need to be the same place where you store your books. Yet houses that are oversized or contain too many rooms can create dysfunction; for instance, a situation where the kitchen is so far away that the user needs a second refrigerator closer to the bedroom. Houses that provide a combination of spaces for solitary or communal activity—whether the community is a family of seven or a single person with a dog—allow

for greater enjoyment of domestic life. Houses also must provide spaces for things as well as people. We are, at times, defined by our possessions. And for most of us, our collections of material goods and devices often exceed our capacity to use them. The goal is for furniture, closets, shelves, and other built-ins to allow us to comprehend and appreciate our possessions, to use them when we need them, put them away when we don't, and understand why we have them.

Once a house is complete, it inevitably will change: its materials weather, its natural and built surroundings shift in scale and condition. People also change, and one cannot predict how they might live in a house over time. A person, like a landscape, comes with a history, yet people possess a self-determined counterpart to the fixity of *terroir* in having character, in desiring and being able to direct their conditions and behavior in terms of their history. The child of a gangster can become a scholar. People cannot change their DNA or their ancestry but they mature and evolve—they experience the world in ways that shape them to be different than their heritage might have dictated. Other change happens whether we want it or not. Children move away, parents become ill, and people fall in or out of love. Everyone ages. A house can adapt, as people do, to new conditions. This can be explicit, in converting a first-floor library into a bedroom to avoid stair climbing, or subtle, in simply appreciating a space anew. You live in the same place for years, your grandchildren come over, and suddenly you're crawling under the furniture for the first time. New activities lead you to see things in different ways. The architect often steps in at this juncture, again, to help form new conditions.

Overall, the important thing is for the house to contain but not inhibit human behavior and development. Despite the basic shared conditions of daily life, you never really know how people actually live. Their individuality distorts the design neutrality at the heart of the house. You know, and yet you don't know. Even in the most generic conditions of housing, individuals will particularize their environment. They shelter or reveal possessions. They display different kinds of art and memorabilia. Some people like color, others don't. Some want hooks instead of shelves. People also diverge in how they do basic things, such as prepare food, stack dishes, or dress. Some people take baths; some take showers. Domestic life contained in a house is profoundly private. People, to the extent to which they control their conditions, show only what they want others to see. So a house, in its dual nature as a neutral structure and a private domain, is a paradox—at once generic and specific, transparent and opaque. Just as the house, in its essentials, is universal, so is the fact that each person occupies a house in particular and mysterious ways.

Rules for Neighbors

RICK MOODY

For about forty years now my family has spent summers on an island off the tip of Montauk called Fishers Island. We started going in the mid-seventies. My father grew up on the Maine coast, and his criterion for a good place to summer with his kids was that the location should resemble Maine but be on the whole more accessible. Indeed, Fishers Island has the same kind of glacial scouring and crosshatching you associate with the Maine coast, and while it's a bit more temperate, and less coniferous, you can see how someone from Maine would want to spend time there. In those days, especially in the houses where we lived in the first couple of years, you could bike to the ocean and not pass but a car or two along the way. Golfing on the little nine-hole course at the cheap end of the island mainly involved driving up with your clubs and walking out to the tee. There were no golf carts.

Gradually, over the course of living for a number of years in an old ramshackle house that had been added onto innumerably, we came to understand that we were the owners of that rarest of things, a Fishers Island house that had *no discernible water view.* Off the back porch, in autumn, when the leaves were strewn about, you could see the barest strip of Connecticut in the distance, including a nuclear power plant. But during the high season, we were up on a hill, somewhat isolated from even the closest neighbors, and there were only maples, a couple of oaks, choke cherry, the stretch of lawn. No view.

The Moodys, therefore, came to be obsessed with this matter of being able to see the water. When I encounter that opening section of *Moby Dick* in which Ishmael talks about the effect of the ocean, I always feel as if he's referring to a like need: *Whenever I find myself growing grim about the mouth; whenever it is a damp, drizzly November in my soul; whenever I find myself involuntarily pausing before coffin warehouses—then I account it high time to get to sea as soon as I can. This is my substitute for pistol and ball.*

One summer, we had heard about a certain hilltop on Fishers Island where there was a water tower, this being, it was said, the highest point on the island, from which you could see off in both directions, ocean and bay. Despite this spot being readily accessible, nobody seemed to have precise directions. We spent the better part of our eight weeks on the island looking for it, turning down each and every dirt road on the East End, sneaking in and around beautiful and stately houses, looking for the fabled, scarcely used, and much rutted track up to the water tower. One day, toward the end of summer, we happened at   last on the road in question. It turned out a bunch of other teens had got there well before us. The tower was heavily graffitied over with instructions for a drinking game.

And yet, the view was incredible. Three-hundred and sixty degrees: Watch Hill, Noank, Groton, New London, Niantic, Old Lyme and Old Saybrook, and then the islands in the Sound, Plum Island, Gardiners Island, Montauk and its lighthouse, ocean, Block Island, ocean, ocean, ocean. Or as we liked to say in those days: *Portugal.* In that direction. Once my brother, sister, and I dragged my father up to see the view, it became even more imperative, a familial ambition, if you will, to find some property on the island that had this promise of limitless expanse, this sense of participation in the immensity of the sea.

As it turned out, about then, the Fishers Island Country Club was selling off a bunch of its holdings. It owned a lot, and it was selling some off. I assume this had to do with tough economic times, and the fact that the FICC was, to a nearly Orwellian degree, controlling every facet of life on the East End (including, e.g., its highly unsavory guardhouse in the middle of the island, designed to keep out *interlopers),* and it could not quite keep up with its ambitions. Among the parcels of land it wanted to shed during this fire sale were ten acres of indigenous thorns and hay that had once been a "ballfield" for the summer employees of the country club. This group of employees included, it is my understanding, or had included at one point, the black caddies who worked at the big golf course back in the day. The ballfield was unused, or had been unused for some time before we got there. Ten acres, for the rock-bottom price of six hundred per. Ten acres, that is, for $6,000. No one seemed to want it but us.

Did I mention that the ballfield was on the road to the best beach on Fishers Island, a dramatic cliff-side spot that was rocky, severe, and with pretty good waves, if that was your thing? The ballfield was within walking distance of that beach. Not a bad place to live, actually. It was my father who got the idea to take a cherry picker out there on the end of the ballfield, where it sloped up, to see if, given a plausible two-story house, dimensions thereof, you could see the water.

And this is where the architecture part comes into it. This is where the story commences to be about some of the issues that are so thoughtfully explored in Deborah Berke's treatise herewith on how to think about architecture and home. My father, upon sitting in the cherry picker at the high end of the property, immediately saw that he could, at last, have his water view, and he conceived of a plan to commission and build on that spot, and to make a self-defined, self-described idea of a home there. An architect was subsequently contracted, a guy who had done quite a number of houses on the island, all of them featuring some fascinating admixture of postmodernism and the old shingle style, the turn-of-the-century look that had dominated the first building boom on Fishers Island, circa 1880.

There were a lot of great things about that house my father and stepmother built. Houses on Fishers Island often have cloying (at one extreme) or very funny (at the other) *names* instead of proper addresses, *Gray Gull* being an example of the one, and *Road View* being the other, and as was often the case with my parents, they bucked the trend and referred to their house as 723, this being the number of the house my stepmom first remembered inhabiting in her childhood. So let's call it 723. It had a big living room on the second floor (not the first floor) with French doors, so you could look out on the whole ballfield (which was converted, let it be said, into horse pasture), it had an enormous deck, facing in the same direction, it had a nice turret/portico on the front, from which, for reasons I never quite understood, small wooden *eggs* dangled ornamentally above the entrance, and later on it had a magnificent guest cottage addition, which increased the long central corridor even more so, into which were inlaid a number of windows of decreasing size to suggest, playfully, the work of perspective in the apperception of house. The house *was* large. Because there was no mortgage

on the property, my parents were free to spend *all the money* on the construction, and they did. The finished building was somewhere north of 5,000 square feet, enough for all of us, and our various spouses and, later, our kids, to fit there, at least for some portion of summer.

But there was one feature that was especially quixotic, even a little provocative. This was the room that we called *the tower.* The tower was basically a third floor, although we insisted at the time that it was really a second-and-a-half floor, just above the library and living room, where you went up a very narrow stair, to a room that had windows on all four sides, and from which, to a degree, you could see the beach, the rocky coastline adjacent to the beach. And the water beyond. Lots of water. The feel in that room was, frankly, like the interior of a Maine lighthouse. It had benches all the way around. It was meditative, and very hot in the summer, good for naps. That room said, without any hesitation or uncertainty, that we could now see the Atlantic. We *definitely* had a water view.

The neighbors, especially the neighbors who had probably been just fine with having an undeveloped ten acre meadow on their road, did not take a shine to the large house that went up in place of the ballfield, not at all. Always and everywhere on Fishers Island it's about the *old familes* and the *new families,* and the whispered critique was about whether the *new families* had just made their money. We failed that test. My grandfather ran a used-car dealership in suburban Massachusetts. A legacy of thrift was mainly what he had passed on.

True, there was the fact that the house was large, even by the standards of a resort community. But nothing was so offensive to the neighbors of Isabella Road, upon which the ballfield was located, as *the tower.* There was a lot of pulling-up-the-ladder-behind-you thinking on Fishers Island, and one manifestation of this habit of thinking was that even though there were a great many third floors on Fishers Island, on the East End, controlled by the ominous, shadowy Fishers Island Development Corporation (a nongovernmental entity that colluded with the country club on its nefarious objectives), no new design was meant to have a third floor, and certainly no new house was meant to have one if the neighbors complained vociferously, especially if among these neighbors was a high-powered lawyer, well situated to malinger.

All that followed was along the lines that have been sketched out in a great many memoirs and nonfiction treatises on the trench warfare of luxury home building, whether in city or country. Lots of upheavals, betrayal by people who promised to support the project, unforeseen support from unlikely quarters, strange bedfellows, nail-biting, and then, when you least suspected, the breaking of ground and the framing up of a new structure.

My father never shrank from a fight. He was an executive in finance when he was still working the nine to five, and he always did what he thought was right no matter the cost to himself personally. When he was president of the *other* country club on Fishers Island, the slightly more democratic club called Hay Harbor, down on the West End, he had overseen the construction of a swimming pool on club property. This was the ultimate in sybaritic, not to say decadent, amenities for those residents who had grown up wearing, one presumes, wool bathing suits, diving into the jellyfish-infested waters of Hay Harbor, eating fish for breakfast, and thinking it was all *good for you.* A number of these folks castigated my father in public, even some who had been his close friends, but he went through with the swimming pool nonetheless, because it was the right thing to do, and now, it's fair to say, the problem with the swimming pool at Hay Harbor is that it's too small.

So he didn't mind tangling with the neighbors over *the tower.* He commissioned the tower and had it built because he thought it was a beautiful design, and because he wanted to be able to see the water, and he got the design through (at least one member of the architecture committee was heard to remark that "this is how design *ought* to look on Fishers Island"), and this curious, idiosyncratic building came to be built, 723.

Building your dream house, as Mr. Blandings once did, as Wittgenstein did, as Jung did, does in fact confer on a person a sense of identity, of the struggle that is individuation, and it makes manifest his or her ideas of home, and that is in part what Deborah Berke means when she says of design that it should *honor daily life.* For my father and my stepmother, a radical turn began with the completion of their house on Fishers Island, in which art and architecture became part of who they were, and what they were about. The daily stuff became easier to do, because of how skillfully the house was made, but the thoughtfulness of the design, and the way, for example, my father collaborated in its most whimsical elements, created an environment in which design and architecture announced their presence, their value, their effectiveness, even though these were lives that had hitherto been concerned with basis points and price-earnings ratios and, lest it seem otherwise, kids.

However, the enmity between ourselves and the lawyer guy across the street persisted. I'm going to say their name was Jennings. The Jennings family *hated* the tower, which admittedly gave a very good view of their front lawn, and front door, and perhaps if you'd used a telescope, their kitchen, etc. They disliked that we had somehow built this house that had a third floor where no third floor was meant to exist on the East End, and they believed, or perhaps it is my extrapolation of their belief, that *more* of this kind of thing was bound to happen, and there goes the neighborhood, or there goes Isabella Road, that wild, untrammeled dirt track on the way to the best beach around.

The animus did not exactly get to anyone in the Moody family. We used to joke about Mr. Jennings, that he was a control *freak,* that he thought he was the major-general of the neighborhood, that he thought no one else should be able to enjoy this part of the island, and so on. I remember I used to do a monologue, with a simulated speech impediment, wherein Mr. Jennings addressed his wife by one of those WASPy pet names, like Pogey or Bitsy, about his need for *sock garters.* I entertained small children with this monologue, *Where are my sock garters? Bitsy, have you misplaced my sock garters?* Not very funny, huh?

To understand the end of the story, in which bitterness dwindles away, you need to know that the Fishers Island Fire Department, all volunteer, and mostly staffed by the year-round population of the island, has not been notable for the number of fires it has extinguished over the years. In fact, to my knowledge, in the modern forty years of my time on Fishers Island, I'm going to say it has *never* quite put out a fire. There have not been many fires to speak of, but when there have been fires, they have normally been of a scale that taxed the all-volunteer fire department of Fishers Island, which you can imagine, on an island of 250 year-round residents (to their credit, they have been *very very* good at ferrying ill people to the mainland in one of those exceedingly fast boats, with 300 horsepower outboard engines, and this is a big deal).

Things therefore did not go well when the Jennings house caught fire. I cannot remember exactly what caused this fire, at all, but I do not think it was a lightning strike, nor was it human foible. I think it was an electrical fire, and that it was just after the season, and so there were not a lot of people around. Once the Jennings house caught fire, there was nothing that could be done to stop it from being consumed entirely, and so the Fishers Island Fire Department tried to make sure that the Jennings fire did not *spread,* and this meant, e.g., wetting down our roof, and the tower, because ours was exactly the direction of the prevailing winds. Smouldering debris, airborne, did come our way, but we were exceedingly lucky. The Jennings family were not. They lost everything and had to start from scratch.

My father came to feel the pain from across the road. It was hard to miss it. And he did the right thing, because that was his way. He offered to let them stay in our house, if they needed to, as long as they needed to. And thus began the thaw. What are the proper rules for conduct with respect to your neighbors, besides that you should do for them as you have them do for you? Additionally, you have to remember that a relationship with a neighbor is never static, that it is always subject to change, and in many cases, these relationships can change *for the better.* For the purposes of this essay, I am going to say that my father's experience in collaborating on the design of his house was coterminous with this recognition of the possibility for change, change for the better. He offered the Jenningses his house, while they got through the beginning of what must have been a long interval of suffering, and even if they did not need this offer, they did presumably appreciate the sentiment.

And then when the Jenningses came to rebuild, we did not stand in the way of their new design, which also featured an attempt to maximize their considerable, and it should be said, very dramatic, view of the beach and coastline. The Jenningses had a magnificent spot, an overpowering spot. When they used the insurance money to rebuild from scratch, they did not duplicate the prior design, they did what my father had done, they made the spot in their own image, and surely they employed, for the great house that they built, the kinds of suggestions that make this book you are holding so wise. For example: *rooms can be outside.* They got a great house out of their adversity.

The longstanding enmity between Jenningses and Moodys came to an end, then, with architecture, and with the pursuit of architecture to maximize the expressive power of landscape, and the relationship between people and space. But allow me one last scene.

It came to pass that I bought a little house on Fishers Island myself, a cottage among those put up by the American military in the first decades of the twentieth century. On the West End. I bought it in 1998, and I used this little house as my writing studio for thirteen years. I therefore was often on the ferry going back and forth from Connecticut, and because, for good or ill, I was not unknown on the island, I was a sitting duck on the ferry boat. One time, for example, I spent an entire boat ride talking to Dana Reeve, the widow of Christopher Reeve, about writing; she was just getting a memoir under way.

And so: I was once approached by a gentle and funny woman on the boat, a woman about my age. I could tell she was *not* a regular Fishers Island type, she wasn't wearing the pastel-colored corduroys, or the golf visor, and she was not in a posse of like-minded libertarians. She was just a regular middle-aged person on the boat, like I was. She was a painter, she told me, and we talked for a bit about creative work on the island, the hardships thereof. You have probably guessed that this painter was the grown daughter of the Jennings family.

I'd had occasion, otherwise, to be friendly with the children of people who had had public disagreements with my dad on the island. I didn't consider it disloyal. I certainly would never have had a conversation that verged on the disloyal. But I did believe that to know these antagonists, and to respect them, was to live in hope, a little bit, that all things were possible when the door was open to dialogue, especially the kind of civilized dialogue that starts with a description of the weather, and moves on to emphasize the little struggles and victories of daily life, and/or let's say, Cézanne. Her name was Sally Jennings, more or less. She was gracious, and she was a great painter, I soon learned, with genuine brush-handling virtuosity and an admirable conceptual streak. And we stayed in touch for a few years (until I left the island, later). She would send me notification of her openings, and I'd run into her on the boat now and then. I considered our acquaintance a triumph.

In part, and this is the epiphanic thought for this essay, I think our acquaintance, the one I've just described, had its origins in ideas about architecture, in the way that harmonious living in the environment over the course of some years takes tribal conflicts *off the table.* Life, it seems, is better given over to questions like: What is the effect of *circulation* on a house? Life is better given over to these questions than to the foreshortenings of pride. And here's how you begin.

RULE ONE: Property lines do not define a site.

RULE TWO: Any material can seduce.

RULE THREE: Repetition elevates the ordinary.

RULE FOUR: Circulation does more than connect.

RULE FIVE: Rooms can be inside, outside, or both.

RULE SIX: Account for all things. Display a few.

RULE SEVEN: Reckon with tradition.

RULE EIGHT: Honor daily life.

RULE ONE:
Property lines do not define a site.

The legal documents of ownership set rules and local regulations for the creation of a house. Exploit these rules in terms of what they cannot limit. Sensuous experiences such as views, breezes, smells, and sounds located beyond legal boundaries are still available. Shrewd considerations of the position and scale of a house can enlarge or otherwise dictate the perceived dimensions and character of a site.

In locating a house, it is almost always best to push out to an extreme edge of the property. This creates a field of space and maximizes advantageous orientations: toward light, water, or an expanse of land; in consideration of trees and other vegetation; in pursuit of quiet or privacy. Rights of way can determine the location but not the experience of entering a property. A hidden, meandering driveway makes a large property feel intimate and a small one expansive. A house that presses against but turns its back to the road seems accessible but paradoxically reveals nothing. Saving information about the property for the entrance into the structure and beyond creates a sequence of surprises.

The impulse to build as high as zoning will allow is not always good. An alternative is to expand horizontally—to lie low—and connect a house to the terrain. Never seek height for its own sake. A second floor could provide invigorating air and astounding views. If the only result is a view of the neighbors, it is better to go flat and create a contained, private world. Inversions of the expected can redefine a site to suit comfort and desire.

A peculiar site is an opportunity. Here, the careful positioning of a house within a narrow triangle appropriates views from an adjacent nature reserve. This borrowing of open public space expands an otherwise squeezed lot and, paradoxically, makes private property feel all the more so.

Find agreement through disobedience. The axis of the house
resists alignment with the triangular site.

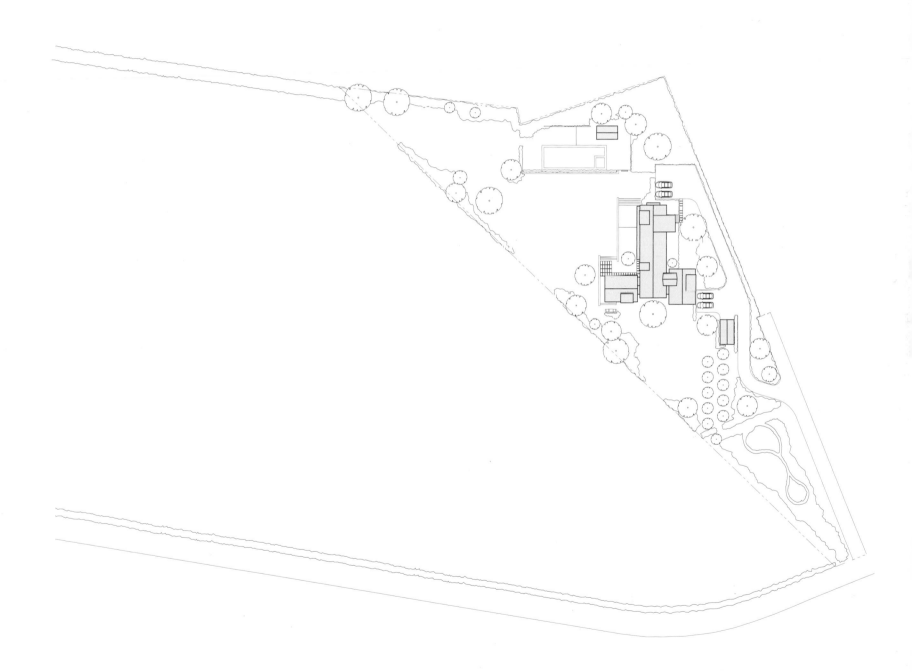

Arrival becomes a journey of mystery and discovery.
Snaking a driveway through a lush and varied landscape gives a
dramatic intimacy to a hundred-acre site. A curving, ascending
approach (determined, in part, by a design choice to cross the
property's many brooks at perpendicular angles) reveals different
views of the house but only at a glance.

Maximize transitions from public to private. A driver entering this property pulls onto a gravel path that curves back to run close, at times parallel, to the main road. Trees and other plantings screen this proximity, however, and the effect is one of immediate delivery into a different space, an expansive realm of sequestered calm.

Stage the landscape. A lowered ceiling frames the kitchen and propels the occupant to move—or just look—toward windows proportioned to capture sweeping views.

OPPOSITE: **Establish proprietary zones.** From inside, a short wall collaborates with long windows to extend the boundary of a room. From outside, it maintains the intimacy of the building. A gentle barrier, it can serve as a bench, and crossing it is easy: just step over. At the same time, it acknowledges that houses—like people—can benefit from having personal space.

A narrow perimeter can be preferable to an open center.
The shallow driveway of this small weekend house seems to merge
with a well-traveled country road. This necessitates a mute facade
that doubles as a fence and also creates surprise: around back, the
house gazes upon two sweeping acres, the luxurious result of having
pushed construction to the edge.

Create boundaries. A series of inward-facing outdoor living spaces declares a new set of property lines that, unlike an open expanse, vary in character. This house, squeezed between two streets and a busy canal, presses to the limits of its trapezoidal plot to establish a site within the site. One space is serene and private; the other, designed for entertaining, is open and flows between two levels.

RULE ONE: Property lines do not define a site.

Sometimes a point, rather than a line, defines a site.
A giant black locust tree anchors and enriches its surroundings.
Its scale speaks to the property's long history of being cultivated.
Its verticality emphasizes the flat rich soil of this former farm.

Lend casual dynamism to an otherwise flat and open site. The owner of this property gradually acquired adjacent and nearby lots to establish an expansive residential compound. Pathways and plantings blur edges between structure and ground, claim relationships among buildings, and create privacy. Long low views exaggerate minimal topographic changes into strong spatial definitions. The original property lines exist on paper but vanish from experience.

Changes in foliage and shading form natural boundaries every bit as real as edge conditions on a map. Even young trees, awkward and lacking individual presence, coalesce like lines in an ink drawing. The screenlike effect sets a visual limit while inviting the eye to move beyond it, affording the experience of a distant edge.

OPPOSITE: A building can anchor a site without overwhelming it.

The loose broken lines of low-lying cobbled walls define a courtyard within separate structures. They delineate areas of repose, play, work, and arrival yet remain open to the rolling countryside. They accommodate the gentle incline of the land with flat spaces that complement steeper slopes.

A simple, stone wall forms its own multifunctional property line. It starts as part of the beach-house foundation, extends to enclose a pool deck, provides elevation for glimpses of the crashing surf, and acts as a threshold delivering you to views beyond.

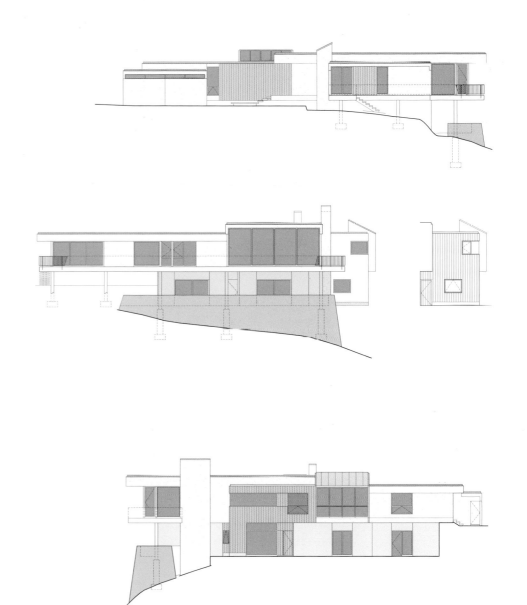

Minor shifts can be potent. Extensive renovation of this midcentury house included adding mahogany boards to the concrete-and-stucco exterior. The resulting moments of deep contrast and texture warm and animate what had been a stark first impression.

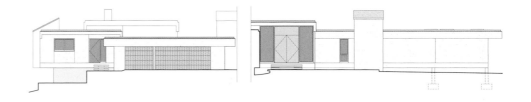

Common, low-cost materials contain sophistication and delight when used with purpose and care. The cedar siding that wraps this small beach house hovers gently above grade and provides an understated contrast to the larger cottages on neighboring lots.

Restraint foregrounds the subtle. The material and color palette of this painting studio sets a stage for proportion and detail, enhancing the verticality of the windows and the thick, flat profile of the baseboard. A dark woodstove punctuates the austerity.

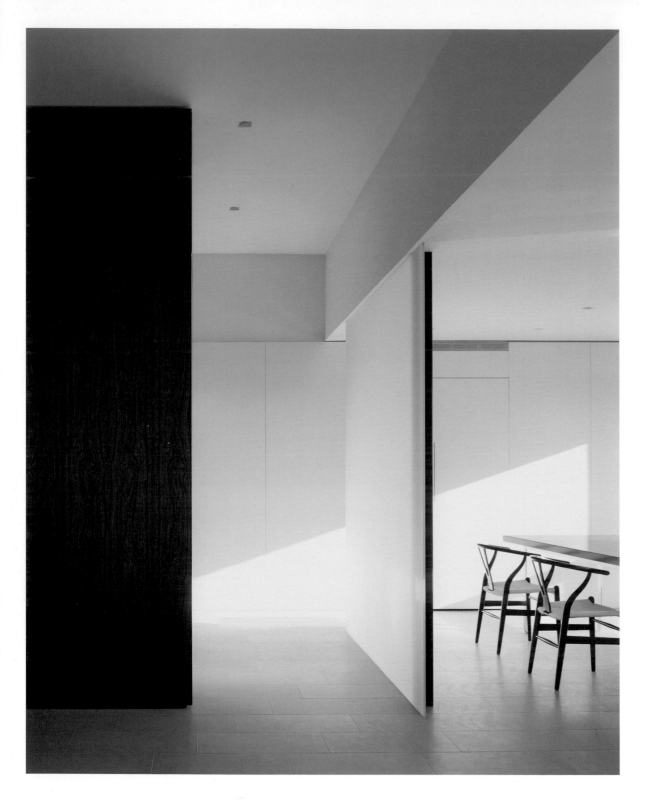

Use materials to dictate the understanding of a space and complement its function. Warm rosewood closets and a frosted-glass partition divide a room and provide textural contrast between bold solidity and a filtered transmission of light.

Seek textural dialogue between architecture and landscape. A brick wall with solid massing and subtle color variation provides a strong counterpoint to the lush plantings that surround it.

OPPOSITE: **Correct positioning creates surprise.** A central fireplace divides a room yet connects the spaces by being open on both sides. Locally sourced New England marble clads the steel structure, a swath of atmospheric gray that softens and complements an austere window grid and overall black-and-white palette.

OPPOSITE: Plain white tile looks fresh and refined next to playful elements.

Find value in existing objects. The rustic charm and rich pattern of former stable doors repurposed for cabinets enlivens a room and contrasts with the smooth consistency of the broad meadow beyond. The doors are installed upside down and inside out relative to their original purpose. The wooden ribbing that once provided reinforcement from kicking hooves now contributes visual texture.

RULE TWO: Any material can seduce.

Attend to the big picture and the close-up. Yellow
Alaskan cedar clads an entire facade, while juxtaposed
zones of horizontal and vertical boards generate variety
within the monochrome—dynamic geometry and sensuous
texture from near and afar.

RULE TWO: Any material can seduce

Reinforce how shadow and light move across and through a variety of surfaces.

OPPOSITE: **Exploit the variety of a single material.** Frosted, etched, clear, and opaque, glass panels play with levels of privacy and visibility. Light diffused from above bounces off a continuous white sheet, deployed on the wall instead of tile for its seamless reflectivity.

A simple material, expressed honestly, can be transcendent.
Used correctly, it can unify indoors and out yet still enliven separate
spaces with specificity. Cladding an entire chimney volume, brickwork
inside surrounds a fireplace with subtle color and tactile warmth.
Outside, it joins a textural conversation among rectangles of wood,
stucco, and shrubbery.

RULE TWO: Any material can seduce.

RULE THREE:
Repetition elevates the ordinary.

Repetition can enliven practical and quotidian forms. A grid of porcelain light sockets resonates in a way that a single socket does not. The rhythmic deployment of identical windows creates a baseline, a backdrop for high notes and variations. The hardware of infrastructure, often an afterthought or a haphazard application, can perform similar music. Switches, vents, or grates arranged in a series or pattern honor their respective uses and create, for the user, a new understanding of their forms: the ordinary gesture of turning on the lights becomes a conscious and therefore pleasurable activity.

The massing of manufactured objects (forty steel cabinets as opposed to four) helps us appreciate our complex relationship with them. Multiples remind us of how things are made, how many things in the world are exactly the same, and how we manage to personalize them. Repetition of use can generate intimacy. There are billions of phones in the world, but yours is yours alone.

Order complements the unpredictable. Windows as a group form a defining exterior band, yet the user's agency to open or shut each one to different degrees disrupts the horizontal to signal the shifting activity of daily life inside.

Divorce sentimental mainstays from storybook associations. Twin gabled roofs challenge the expectations of New England white clapboard, as do sets of windows that repeat the same vertical proportions to varied effect—oversized, minimized, clustered, and isolated. On the second floor, a screened porch is a deliberate and intimate destination, especially in contrast to the porch located, more traditionally, on the ground floor. Together, these intermediary zones between inside and out offer contexts for a range of occasions and moods, from entertaining guests to relaxing alone.

RULE THREE: Repetition elevates the ordinary.

OPPOSITE: **Repetition accommodates variety.** Syncopated rhythms of form, texture, light, and shadow form a dynamic patchwork that animates and unifies a vast facade.

Intangibles create drama. Often unnoticed, roof slats express themselves through dramatic shadow. Stripe-and-lozenge configurations shift as they travel across the different materials, from wood-plank walls to stone floor to any surrounding furniture. Though fleeting, the pattern becomes a recognizable unit. Seen up close or from across the pool, it signals—and makes the user more aware of—the weather and time of day. Bright sun forms crisp lines and details. Clouds make patches of more or less defined geometry. And because the pattern vanishes, a sense of anticipation can develop around the ordinary yet unpredictable changes that elicit its reappearance.

Necessity yields elegance. Owners planned to convert this house, eventually, into a garage. Their intention determined the spacing and scale of doors and windows to match future garage bays, giving a temporary solution a bold and pleasing facade.

RULE THREE: Repetition elevates the ordinary.

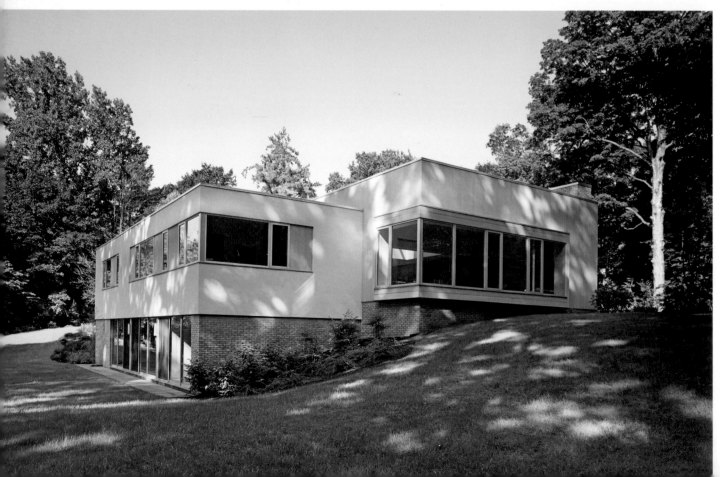

OPPOSITE: **Let nature serve as a foil to structure.**
Nested within a rolling topography, repeated volumes
take on a dynamic rhythm of sameness.

Think in terms of sets and units. A nearly square glass pane
repeats to create three different window forms. The smallest, made
of four panes, doubles to create the windows that multiply along the
ground floor. Evenly spaced, these long rectangles and the identical
widths of the shingled interstices create a uniform backdrop for a
jutting dormer. This wood-clad form is further distinguished by its
bold window—the largest "set" of glass units—yet it connects to
the rest of the facade by its showcasing of the smallest four-by-four
configuration. Starting with something simple allows for infinite
variations that lead to balance and complexity.

RULE THREE: Repetition elevates the ordinary.

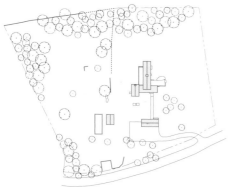

Repetition can be momentary. Each of these three gabled volumes is identical in its roof pitch, louvered grill, and shingled cladding, but this deliberate rhyming is apparent only from certain vantage points on the property. When it snaps into focus, the symmetry enacts a visual "happening" that grounds a romantic composition in a palpable rigor.

Repetition can create texture. White vertical boards separated by crisp shadow lines wrap rooms in a rich pattern that layers and unites volumes of space. A thin wall remains distinct while joining an expanse that incorporates the stairway hall and dining room.

Emphasize the modular. Spaced and clustered with care, windows that are different appear to be arrangements of the same unit. The small upper-floor rectangles repeat across the facade, gathering into a contained, dormered grid before moving below and multiplying into a window row. The stone wall and shingled roof emphasize this horizontality: the similar patterning of different materials forms a line that holds the eye. Offsetting the flow are stone chimneys that match the wall below—they punctuate the overall effect with a vertical pop.

RULE THREE: Repetition elevates the ordinary.

Grids create order, they do not impose it. Wood slats combine with a steel frame to define and shade a space, but the regularity does not overwhelm. On the contrary, the structure recedes—it is present and ephemeral, there and not there.

OPPOSITE: **Notice structure.** When showcased, workaday beams, rafters, and joists become design elements.

RULE THREE: Repetition elevates the ordinary.

Fields of color stage moments of repetition. Doors and trim pop within an overall red exterior. Inside, yellow becomes a dynamic backdrop for shifting light through a window grid, its hue growing duller or brighter in contrast to the changing rectangles of color from outside.

Repetition unifies new and old. The forms and textures of this house take cues from existing Civil War–era barns, adopting the historical style of wood cladding but flipping it from vertical to horizontal. Additions look organic. Traditional forms look fresh.

RULE FOUR:
Circulation does more than connect.

Moving through and around a house is usually about reaching a destination or getting something done. Those journeys can be productive, but they should never be automatic or dull. The route from one place to another must be active. It requires respect and awareness. Pathways should enrich comfort not by making a house feel more familiar but by highlighting how it changes. Corridors and rooms should enhance the experience of the time of day, the time of year, and even the weather. This can happen not only visually, with windows that draw shifts of light, but also audibly, with materials that enhance sounds such as rain overhead or gravel underfoot. Occupants should be conscious of their physical relationship to the space—their shoulders to the walls, for example. They also should feel stimulation and comfort from sensing the relationship between the space they inhabit and the surrounding environment.

The trip from one space to another can be episodic. These moments can be as simple as passing a window or pausing on a landing. They can be social. Pathways through a house should create opportunities for connection, whether that means stopping to interact with the people around you or slowing to see what others are doing. Equally important are opportunities for solace and reflection, for thinking, looking, or simply being.

Awareness increases the pleasure of occupying a house and makes life more complex. Connection is a job. Circulation is an experience.

Facilitate connection in multiple directions. A rolling ladder moves up, down, and sideways to give the user agency. It creates a shortcut between first and second floors. It provides access to hard-to-reach storage. Black geometry floating against a white background, the ladder activates the room as a functional yet compositional object, something meant to be seen and positioned to advantage.

OPPOSITE: **Scale circulation to create intimacy.** Low-rise steps form a subtle yet distinct shift from hallway to bedroom.

Afford discovery. Openings both reveal and conceal what lies ahead on a path from gravel parking court through narrow garage to grassy front yard, where the ultimate destination—the house entryway—hides in deep shadow. Inside the garage, two small doorknobs hint at cross-axial circulation between a studio workshop on the left and a storage shed on the right. Once the exterior panel slides shut, circulation is contained to the private sphere of a domestic compound.

OPPOSITE: Movement into and through a house accelerates and collects, like a stream with eddies.

Allow for mystery. A roof structure orients visitors toward a front door that is barely distinguishable from a matching wood wall. This undifferentiated surface shifts attention to visual modes of access to the house, through windows, and provides a surface for the play of light and shadow.

Establish opportunities for ritual. To enter this modest beach house, the user must park in the garage and traverse a gravel courtyard. This short walk from car door to front door—after a long drive from the city—affords an opportunity to transition from outside to in, from one state of mind to another.

The most efficient arrival is rarely the most pleasurable.
A meandering driveway tempers speed and invites sensual enjoyment.

A stair landing offers an inside encounter with a bold red exterior. The arresting view reminds the user of the horizontality of the house and encourages a moment for pause and reflection.

Conceal circulation for privacy
and elements of surprise.

From an outdoor gathering space, the ocean is an ephemeral presence, accessible via smell and sound. But the house gives the user visual clues about how to get there physically. Ahead, a pathway leads over the dunes to the beach. Above, a railing signals an upper deck with a majestic view.

OPPOSITE: **A simple glassed entryway becomes a property's central node.** From outside, it offers glimpses into and through the house. From inside, it showcases the landscape and leads left or right, connecting and separating public and private spaces.

A view invites circulation.

Acknowledge transitions. A step and overhang create a space both indoors and out, a resting place between the glassed doors of a porchlike room to a path that wraps the entire house and connects multiple structures on the property.

OPPOSITE: **Create anticipation.** The descent into a pool begins well above the water line.

Circulation expands a threshold. A path from parking court to front door passes a bedroom window for a glimpse of interior warmth before it reaches the entrance.

Deny hierarchy. A curved driveway at first suggests a grand arrival for visitors, or occupants, being dropped off at the door. Close inspection reveals a path of concrete pavers that intersects the gravel, a gesture that celebrates travel by foot and vehicle alike. The shift in texture, visible and tactile, delineates types of circulation and honors each.

Control movement to suit the occasion. When open, sliding glass doors encourage casual access between kitchen and dining areas. When closed, they focus attention on events in one space or the other, at the stove or the table. Regardless, visual circulation remains active.

OPPOSITE: Unexpected glimpses of circulation hint at spaces not immediately apparent.

RULE FIVE:
Rooms can be inside, outside, or both.

Simple distinctions between indoors and outdoors are artificial and wrongly polarized. What constitutes a room has dozens of iterations made up of an infinite range of flavors and qualities. "Inside" and "outside" are best understood as ends of a spectrum in the relationship between structure and landscape.

A room can nestle in the terrain or hover over it. A room can have walls and no roof or a roof and no walls. An allée of trees makes a leaf-covered room. Windows, entryways, breezeways, foyers, porches, patios, decks, courtyards, and thresholds of all kinds: such zones need not be mundane. With careful consideration, they become active, fluid, and complex. They allow for agency: the users can tune spaces to their needs, sensibilities, and surroundings.

At essence is a balance between shelter and exposure. Comfort lies in liberation as well as protection, in being open to a view and concealed from being on view. A spectrum between inside and out operates in tandem with a spectrum of mood. Different kinds of rooms provide opportunities to search out surroundings to either reinforce or transform a state of mind. Spatial sameness denies the complexity of everyday life.

Appropriate the outdoors. The glass surrounding a living area melts away to let the landscape rush in, transforming a traditional room with a view into a complex space where the room is the view. A shallow balcony functions as an intermediary zone between structure and nature, accessed by doors located on the side to maintain the immateriality of the frontal window wall. The occupant can project herself visually to occupy the exterior space, regardless of whether she goes there.

A pool can be a room, its sunken rectangular area emphasized by the edges of surrounding structures. Different levels create horizontal stages of entry. Steps lead from the house terrace to a shade pavilion that sits just above the water, making that perfect flat glistening plane yet another level for access. The effect is one of rooms within rooms that shift by degree from contained to open.

RULE FIVE: Rooms can be inside, outside, or both.

Use light to dematerialize the solid. Contrast between shade and sun penetrates the heart of a house and diminishes the interior in favor of the outdoors. This reversal accentuates the stone patio, making it even more of a room in its own right.

Deploy different sliding elements
depending on weather, time of day,
season, or occasion.

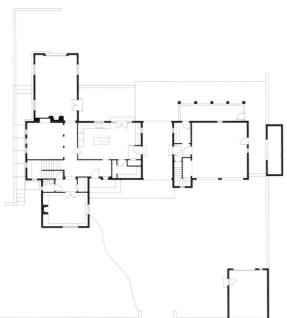

Thresholds stage a narrative. Concentric zones become more intimate as they scale from public to private, from property line to courtyard to breezeway. But then, the rhythm inverts. A yard opens up behind the house, spacious but enclosed.

Materials create continuity.

Rhyme linear elements to create sequence and connection.
Horizontals cohere into movement from work surface to ventilation
hood to window to horizon. A panoramic view meets intimate activity.
Eyes connect with hands. Thoughts project into nature.

Engage the senses. The sound and feeling of gravel underfoot provide a distinctly exterior experience, even as the surrounding courtyard walls create a sensation of interiority. A sound can signify the outdoors as much as the sight of a tree.

OPPOSITE: **Invert expectations of defined space.** Oversize sliding doors dematerialize an interior flanked by crisp landscaping. Dense plantings edge the gravel floor of a courtyard, while a distant wall of foliage brackets an expansive lawn. The contrast makes a dining area seem more like an interstitial opening between outdoor rooms.

RULE FIVE: Rooms can be inside, outside, or both.

Sequence the view. Inside the house, a ceiling that rises from low in the dining room to higher in the living room leads the user toward a vista framed by the gradation of louvers, patio, and canopy.

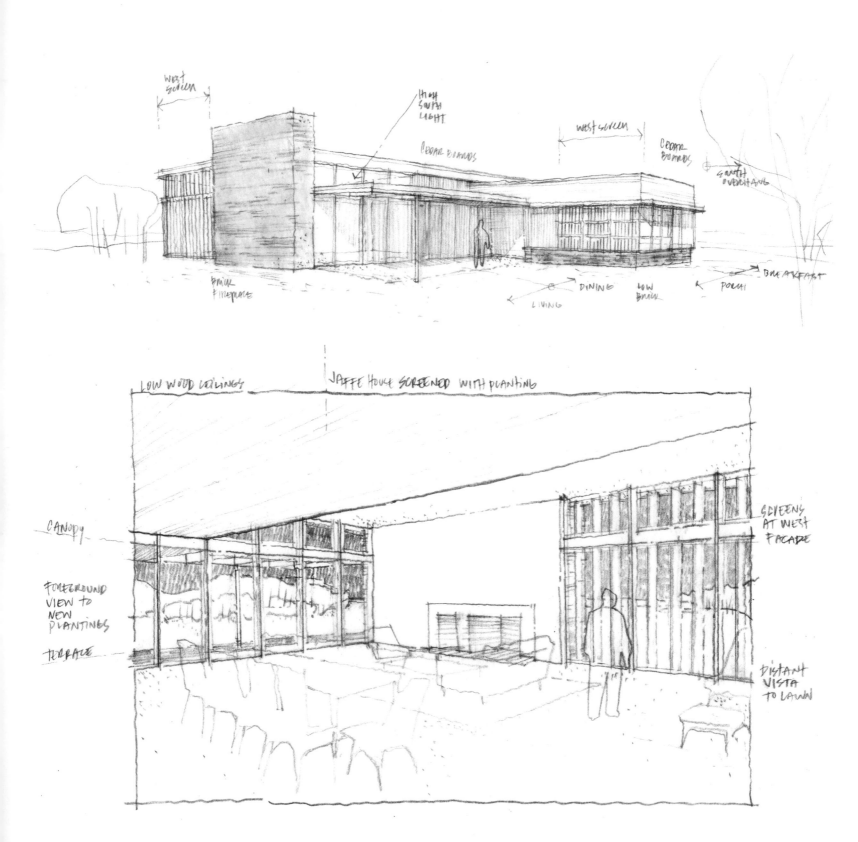

Compression accentuates the expansive.

Sun streaming through a *brise-soleil* allows a narrow entryway to breathe. Parallel shadows echo the verticality of the cedar boards overhead.

RULE FIVE: Rooms can be inside, outside, or both.

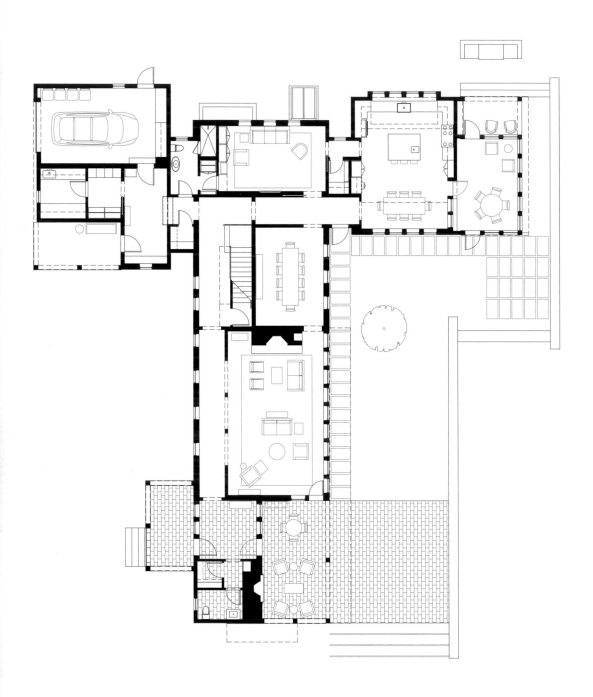

A floor plane can slip through a house, delivering visitors from front yard to back. Here, a bluestone surface travels from outside to inside and back out again, where views open up to the ocean.

RULE FIVE: Rooms can be inside, outside, or both.

OPPOSITE: **Interstitial zones can occur anywhere.** The doorjamb of this room within a room carries a bold shift in palette from the glossy white master bath. It forecasts rosewood walls but retains its own identity.

Play with opposites. Reflective materials animate and enlarge a cocoonlike, intimate space. Solid forms float and multiply in a sea of glossiness. With coy deliberation, a single transparent band punctures the sense of enclosure and brings in the landscape.

RULE FIVE: Rooms can be inside, outside, or both.

An experience of arrival should precede the entrance.
Textural shifts between ground cover and a hard-lined courtyard create stages of approach to this L-shaped house. A winding driveway through woods and meadow affords an episodic journey from the natural to the cultivated to the built. The groomed yet wild-seeming long grass emphasizes the geometry of the parking area as an outdoor room—one that paves the way, in every sense, to the indoor foyer and the rooms beyond.

Consider the occupant's eye level.

Subvert the relationship between floor plane and ground plane. Generous windows and custom furniture nestle this porch in a sloping site. To sit in this room is to sit in the landscape.

RULE FIVE: Rooms can be inside, outside, or both.

Glass is not the only way to merge inside and out. A unified wood palette on walls and floor melds a screened porch with the scenery beyond. Modest windows that emphasize the interior and frame the exterior create a visual connection between a building material and its natural source.

OPPOSITE: **Thresholds of all kinds signal entry.** A shade structure forms an external foyer that invites a moment of pause and frames a view of the door. With a sense of anticipation, the experience of the house starts well before the user walks inside.

RULE FIVE: Rooms can be inside, outside, or both.

Make the view an event. Cedar bleachers extend from a
screened porch to create a zone for lounging that nods to
spectatorship—the enjoyment of observing outdoor activities,
in solitude or with company. Sometimes a room doesn't need
to be more than a platform raised from the ground plane.

Invert associations of inside and out. A barn door usually appears on the exterior of a building. Here, it physically separates an artist's studio from the rest of a house and symbolically signals the boundary between work and home. Conversely, the door—really a sliding wall—can open to welcome in the domestic and social. Yet even when opened up, the studio maintains its feeling of exteriority with a direct path to the outside.

Distinguish degrees of enclosure. Framed by the solid walls
of a guest wing, a pool yard becomes a roomlike retreat, a haven
from the hectic street and the busy canal visible through a generous
breezeway that functions as yet another zone of enclosure, one
shaded yet open to the sky above and the water beyond.

Even subtle gestures provide direction. A coral stone floor and concrete overhang define a waterfront patio. The roof gives shelter, yet its delicate form expresses movement up and out, toward views of a lush landscape.

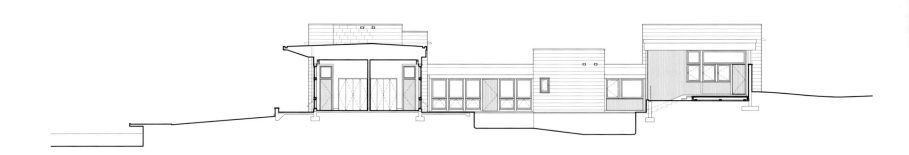

Some outdoor rooms facilitate
a diversity of programs.

OPPOSITE: Others accommodate specific activities.

RULE SIX:
Account for all things. Display a few.

Calmness and peace come from spaces clear of unnecessary objects. Ordered storage allows for control and accounting of what we possess.

Some things we store need to be accessible on a daily basis, such as pots and pans, linens, or clothing. This can be seasonal: with summer, we put away the down comforter and get out the cotton blanket. Other things need to be hidden yet reachable, such as electrical cords and printers. Storage also exists in symbiosis with display, a strategy with subtle applications. Someone with five equally loved paintings and one ideal wall can choose to hang a different painting at different times and thus change the character of a space.

The inverse of selective display is mass display. The owner of a thousand books will not put two hundred in five different rooms. Similarly, the collector of vintage toys wants to appreciate these objects in conversation with one another. Depth of display reveals the richness of thoughtful accumulation.

At the same time, keeping the good china in a ministorage unit for special occasions probably indicates too much china. The ability to see quantity is a control mechanism; it provides a reference point for tracking amount and location. The value of possessions lies in the agency to deploy, employ, and enjoy them. Ideally, we own things in order to use them.

Convenient storage need not announce its presence.
A floor-to-ceiling rosewood partition separates living room
from entry while providing ample space behind its flush doors.

Employ hardware like punctuation.

Treasured objects receive site-specific
architectural recognition.

Storage can accommodate—even frame—disorder.

OPPOSITE: **Details suggest display; display becomes a detail.** Wainscoting presents a line for art that doubles as an architectural frieze.

Emphasize zones of openness and enclosure. The austere front facade of this property—a wooden expanse with a few punched windows—sets up the surprise of a back volume, hidden from the front, that lays it all out.

Tune mood to usage. Screenlike, doors slide for utility or hospitality. Closed, they offer privacy and compel with mystery, hinting at activity on the other side. Storage here conceals itself: the identical treatment of the wooden panels hides the presence of a garage.

Conceal or reveal.
Closed white millwork cabinets blend with the walls, protecting rare ceramics from the curious hands of grandchildren. Open, they rest flush to present a treasured collection accented by a mirrored backdrop.

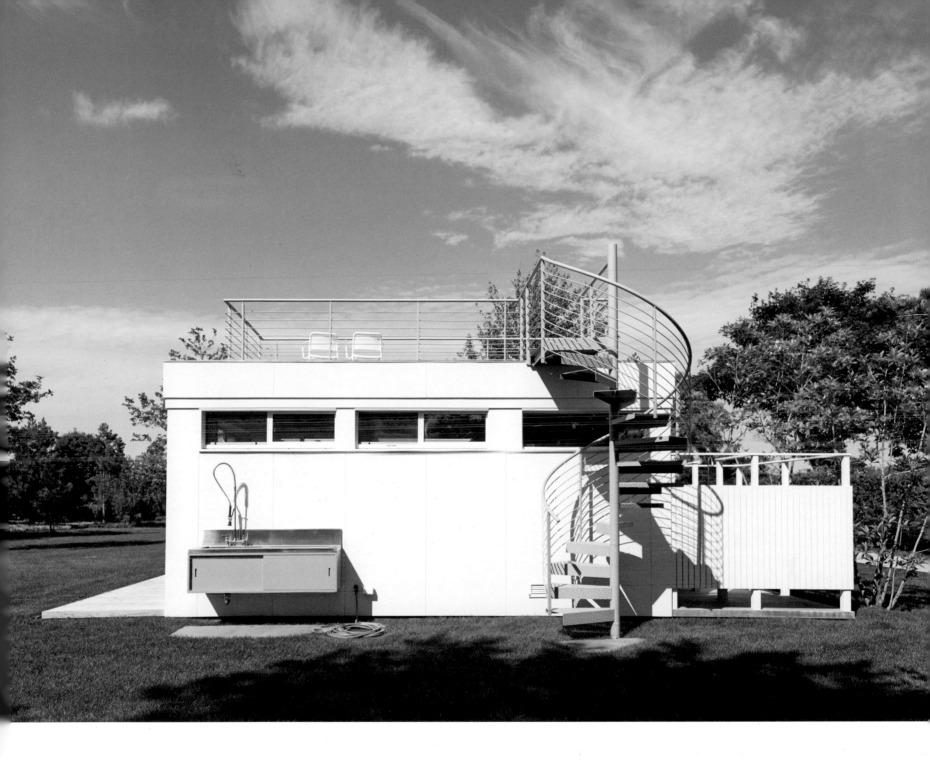

Celebrate function. Exposed and industrial, this vegetable garden sink and storage unit coheres with the adjacent architecture yet gives playful nods to its purpose. An acid chartreuse cabinet suggests the color of plants. A stainless-steel faucet curves like a reed. An ordinary green rubber hose transcends ubiquity to achieve exuberance.

RULE SIX: Account for all things. Display a few.

RULE SEVEN:
Reckon with tradition.

To reckon with tradition is to strike a balance between kneejerk rejection and unconsidered embrace of conventional forms and materials. Context and location help determine these decisions. A house in a dense community surrounded by pitched roofs might have a flat roof yet be clad in the same clapboard as its neighbors. On the other hand, a house on an open mountainside takes it cues from the area's climate and resources.

Architectural traditions also converse with social traditions. Are showers or baths preferred? Is food cooked or ordered out? Are meals on the run or rituals for gathering? What holidays are celebrated and how? Outdoor activities are traditions that determine the circulation of a house and the number and location of doors. Is it desirable to feel open to the elements or better to experience the house as an inviolate shelter? Are there dogs, cats, or other animals, and do they sleep inside?

Beyond these questions lie shifting expectations, via technology, between what a house looks like and how it functions. Spaces once devoted to distinct activities, such as reading or music, lose their purpose when screens of all kinds isolate one kind of experience and expand others. Rooms such as the kitchen need to expand beyond their original function to become common spaces where people can perform different activities yet also be together.

Innovate with old-fashioned forms. A high base wall presses oversize double-hung windows up under a shed roof that tilts at a jaunty angle. This counterintuitive line points to the entryway, which opens and dematerializes a typically solid corner.

Foil tradition with sentimental details in unexpected places. A shedlike facade intersects with a structure reminiscent of a schoolhouse. White trim jettisons its decorative nature and becomes an element of graphic composition.

RULE SEVEN: Reckon with tradition.

Mess with the regional. A Hudson Valley house prods the familiar elements of gabled roof and dormer window. Wood siding tucks under to form a rectangular window zone. The shallow overhang draws lines with shadow, echoing and emphasizing other geometry across the facade.

Traditions are pliable. An addition to this midcentury-modern home works within the parameters of its original forms but eschews the severity of stucco for the warmth of mahogany and the regularity of a uniform window wall for a playful variety of window types.

Compose with contrasts. The typical—a wood-clad second floor with evenly spaced windows—rests atop a ground floor atypical for its band of windows. The mix creates a light-filled downstairs and a private upstairs. From the exterior, it looks like a conventional building landed on a rule breaker.

Functional considerations lead to design surprises.
Sheltering a single wall-mounted light next to the door creates
an intriguing asymmetry, echoed by the steps below. A gutter
downspout accentuates cedar boards and white trim, providing
piping—both literal and figurative—at the volume's edge.

Combine vernaculars. Galvanized metal roofing, stained wood shingles, and gabled roofs signal functionality within a distinctly modern three-part composition. Each volume houses a different program, from entry to living and sleeping, and they interlock in an open, casual array of spaces. The industrial palette and atypical window arrangements make a barnlike structure feel new and fresh.

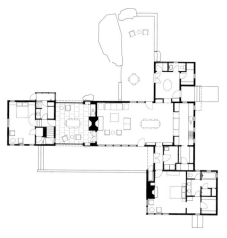

RULE SEVEN: Reckon with tradition.

Paradoxically, an embrace of one tradition showcases the rejection of others. An exuberant allover application of New England–barn red draws attention to nontraditional massing and details like an asymmetrical facade and extended garage roof. In an inverse color move, a brilliant yellow upends East Coast traditions of porch ceilings painted in cool pastels.

Context jolts expectations.
The traditional aspects of a
Long Island beach home
dominate from a distance but
recede on approach. Modern
geometrical elements, like a
spare white overhang and
rectangular pavers, take over,
and, suddenly, a strip of
weathered brown shingles
commands attention.

Be graphic. Gleaming white boards against an orderly backdrop of gray shingles and double-hung windows tweak convention in the context of historic eastern Long Island. White trim becomes a white door, a white window, a white wall.

Traditions are personal. Sweeping terrain has deep meaning for owners who acquired adjoining parcels to accommodate a love of outdoor activity, be it reading in the shade, tossing Frisbee with the kids, or running with the dog. Floor-to-ceiling windows integrate the horizon into the house, a reflection of how a family inhabits a property inside and out.

RULE SEVEN: Reckon with tradition.

Flout design norms. Color and proportion subvert conventional treatments of structural and finishing elements on a beachside studio. The roof tie under a pitched roof extends downward with legs that support a stairway. Multiple skinny columns (as opposed to a few broad ones) take cues from the narrow site, turning awkwardness into an asset. Staining a horizontal wood support beam the same gray as the vertical siding connects different uses of a single material. Simple gestures become complex in their refusal to code building components according to purpose.

Exaggerate. A wood ceiling becomes a featured surface, upending notions of where to apply finishes or decor.

Bring outside elements indoors. A hallway opening turns the living room into a view. Multiple steps of varied depth frame double windows with a richness that goes far beyond function. The effect is an emphasized moment of surprise—an opening in the wall is also an articulated sculptural experience. The choice to double the window provides an inside reminder of what happens outside, where windows of similar dimensions cover the facade.

OPPOSITE: The charm of simplicity and symmetry produces unexpected results.

RULE EIGHT:
Honor daily life.

Provide for moments of relaxation and social occasion.

OPPOSITE: Consider morning routines and the orientation of spaces toward natural light.

Embrace the experience of time. Materials can improve with age. A house should strengthen with the inevitabilities of climate and season.

Accommodate visitors. Shaping a driveway with landscaping gives a guest wing connected to the house a sense of separation and privacy. The clear curve guides arrival and the crisp rectangular edge near the garage signals a designated spot for one more car.

Engage the local. A wall of indigenous stone reclaimed from excavation elsewhere reminds the user of the character and activities of a specific place.

OPPOSITE: **Defer to the terrain.** A main entrance showcases natural rolling topography, allowing for everyday appreciation of how the site slopes in relation to flat farmland in the distance.

Cultivate intimacy outdoors. The judicious removal of a few trees carves out a space for enjoyment. Tucked into the corner of the property, this pool is not a focal point but an exalted surprise. A landscape can hug you.

Seek a view.

Bring joy to arrival. A red door carries happy associations across cultures, be it protection from evil, celebration of prosperity, a welcome to visitors, or a sign that those who enter will find nurture and rest inside. It follows that such a positive hue can have diverse applications. On a sweeping shingled facade, the door collaborates with a low porch overhang and pavers spaced to the human step to establish an intimate, cottagelike scale. Nestled in the shadows of wood-clad rectilinear masses, bold color beams out from the end of the walkway to signal destination. Both houses have similarities, yet the red door looks specific to each.

Facilitate productivity
and daydreaming.

OPPOSITE: Be outdoors.

Embrace the interstitial. A porch accommodates movement between indoor and outdoor activities. The user can pause to rest or sit and relax.

Scale furniture to comfort and use. Designed for the room, this table dignifies modest proportions and simple details.

OPPOSITE: **Certain spaces are best saved for specific times of day.** An outdoor dining patio plays host to the afternoon light and welcomes all to enjoy the last rays of summer sun.

Ease the transitions of departure
and arrival.

Enter nature.

Afterword

MARC LEFF

I am sure it's obvious to everyone that, when designing a house, we don't refer to a list of strict principles. In fact, the entire premise of this book is a bit tongue-in-cheek, because the "house rules" laid out in these pages don't exist to guide our work as if they were eight unbreakable commandments. We don't follow them like a recipe or formula. And we don't lord them over our clients: "I'm sorry, you can't have a separate refrigerator and freezer here—that violates Rule Three!"

Before thinking about this book, we never even considered that there might be rules underlying our work. We just knew that, going on a few decades now, we have been designing houses for some very different personalities in a wide range of places—the country, the beach, the suburbs, the mountains, and the city. And to an outside observer, those projects might seem to be all over the map in more than just geographical terms. There are pitched roofs, flat roofs, small punched windows, big expanses of glass, and countless other variations. So, we asked ourselves, why do these houses feel so consistent and similar to us, besides the fact that we know them so intimately? It had to be more than mere familiarity.

As we pinned up photos and drawings of long-completed projects alongside more recent ones, it became evident that what unified these houses into a single body of work wasn't anything outward—say, a favorite material or repeated motif—but something inward. The consistency resided in our convictions and thinking as architects.

So it seems that these rules have always existed within the collective mind of our practice. We've just never expressed them quite so explicitly (and emphatically). Whether deciding how a house should sit on the land or how to deploy a piece of wood, we have always been guided by the considerations spelled out in this book. Occasionally, the guidance we give our clients even has a tinge of morality, as when we talk about a design being right or wrong. So, in the end, "rules" seems appropriate.

But we are not dictators, and we realize that a house can be a deeply personal thing for our clients. They, not we, are going to live there. So these rules function more like guiding strategies or even meaningful starting points. They're always in the back of our minds as a conversation leads to a sketch that grows into a full-blown design, and a new house gets built.

Along the way, we suggest, urge, and persuade. But we also listen, imagine, and put ourselves in someone else's shoes. Like all good rules, the ones described in this book, I think, are nuanced enough and sufficiently vague to give us all the loopholes we need. Rather than binding us by annoying dos and don'ts, the rules lead to a design process that is full of surprise and delight.

I remember Deborah once explaining to a client how it would be dishonest to put timber beams that had no structural purpose whatsoever across the gabled ceiling of a large, open living room. (And I'm not sure that our client had ever considered that the design of a ceiling had such a weighty moral imperative as truth and honesty.) Far from being a conversation about limits, it was one about possibilities and the impetus to invent new ways to highlight the scale, proportion, and materiality of a great room. I think that client is as happy as we are about the result. It is a space not only devoid of clichés, but also like no other. It is a product of our house rules.

Acknowledgments

It took the efforts and support of many people to make this book, and many others joined forces to realize the projects documented within it. To everyone who has worked for and with Deborah Berke Partners over the years, thank you.

Within the DBP office, I am grateful for the creative talents of architects and designers including my partners Mait Jones and Marc Leff; senior principals Caroline Wharton Ewing and Stephen Brockman; principals Catherine Bird, Noah Biklen, Ameet Hiremath, Rhoda Kennedy, and Terrence Schroeder; senior associates Arthi Krishnamoorthy and Chris Yost; and associates Chad Broussard, Gabriel Ce, Christopher Kitterman, Andrew Ledbetter, Brendan Lee, and John Midgette. A list of employees is on page 204; additional thanks to everyone named there.

I would like to acknowledge all of our clients for their faith in our vision and our "rules"—we have all learned from you. To the clients whose houses appear in this book, a special thanks.

The book itself could not have been achieved without the enormous efforts of Miko McGinty, Anjali Pala, Scott Parks, Tal Schori, Anne Thompson, and Matt Zuckerman. I am very grateful for the intelligence and dedication they brought to the project. I thank the novelist Rick Moody for contributing a wonderful essay and Amy Hempel for introducing me to him. We also are grateful to all the photographers who have documented our buildings over the years, in particular those whose work is included here.

Finally, a special thanks to my husband, Peter McCann, and my daughter, Tess McCann. Their ongoing support is essential in everything I do.

Project Index

Employee List

Emily Abruzzo	Jennifer Carruthers	Anna Finneran
Chardae Adams	Gabriel Ce	Yelenyn Garcia
Katherine Adams	Elizabeth Chadkin	Doris Garner
William Agostinho	Emily Chaffee	Glenn Garrison
Emily Alford	Stephanie Christoff	Tala Gharagozlou
Sarah Anderson	Roberto Cipriano Jr.	Michael Glassman
Damaris Arias	Brandon Dean	Graham Gordon
Elena Baranes	Michael Decker	Margaret Gorman
Madeline Barnhard	Marina de Conciliis	Virginia Gray
Deborah Berke	Janette Delfin	Martha Hagen-Black
Alper Besen	Joeylynn Demeo	Gregory Haley
Noah Biklen	Kiki Dennis	Kelsey Handelman
Logan Billingham	Elie Derman	Christopher Harnish
Catherine Bird	Jennifer Duhamel	David Hettler
Benjamin Bischoff	Sarah Durfee	Matthew Hettler
Alan Brake	Shavon Durham	Eliza Higgins
Zachary Brennan	Katherine Dyke	Jason Hill
Patricia Brett	Julie Eakin	Ameet Hiremath
Stephen Brockman	Katherine Eberly	Sarah Holton
Chad Broussard	Olivia Eckfeld	Shirley Hsu
Gunnar Burke	Irene Fagan	Margaret Hu
Daniel Burkhardt	Ilsa Falis	Richard Irving

Jean Jaminet
Karilyn Johanesen
Whitney Johnson
Jonathan Jones
Maitland Jones
Ryan Keiper
Matthew Kelley
Rhoda Kennedy
Dasha Khapalova
Melanie Kim
Christopher Kitterman
Arthi Krishnamoorthy
Anne Kuruc
Stephanie Lam
Stephen Lam
Stephane Le Blanc
Andrew Ledbetter
Brendan Lee
Marc Leff
Amy Lelyveld
Maynard Leon
Shirley Leong
Marissa Levin
Yi Chen Li
Peter Liao
Cara Liberatore
Meredith Lovejoy
Richard Mandimika
Georgette Maniatis
Mario Marchant
Emily Martyn
Erin McCormick
Andrew McGee
Elizabeth McLendon
Emily Meza

John Midgette
Daniel Montalvo
Jacquelyn Moore-Hill
Jennifer Moye
Mary Kate Murray
Simon Murray
Nathan Nagai
Christina Nastos
Thao Nguyen
Melissa Nosal
David O'Brien
Joshua Padgett
Jenny Pantaleon
Melanie Pantaleon
Scott Parks
Jessie Poksa
Aaron Plewke
Daniel Pontius
Alessandro Preda
Scott Price
Stephani Resch
William Reue
Jenna Ritz
Danielle Roberts
Melissa Rodriguez
Christopher Romero
Faith Rose
Michelle Rossomando
Jennifer Schiffer
Tal Schori
Karina Schroeder
Terrence Schroeder
Robert Schultz
Jake Sigal
Michael Signorile

Heather Snyder
David Sobol
Janine Soper
Stephanie Spoto
Bradley Stephens
Courtney Stern
Alexander Stinchcomb
Jonathan Swendris
Alex Tailer
Maki Takenouchi
Yasemin Tarhan
Karina Tengberg
Ayanna Thomas
Bronwen Thomas
Caleb Todd
Kieran Trihey
Tom Tulloch
Renee Vanegas
Simon Vargas
Joan Vasciana
Ashley Verbanic
Kate Warren
Jane Wechsler
Grzegorz Weglarski
Lindsay Weiss
Caroline Wharton Ewing
Duncan White
Janisha Wilson
Tianwei Ye
Katrina Yin
Christopher Yost
Shuning Zhao
Matthew Zuckerman

Photography Credits

David de Armas: 170 bottom
Jane Beiles: 61, 90, 182 bottom
Eric Boman: 53, 99, 163 right, 185
Chris Cooper: title page, 12, 14, 31, 64, 65, 100, 107, 132, 148, 188, 189, 191 bottom, 193
Deborah Berke Partners: 147, 162, 174
Gentl & Hyers: 51 bottom, 195
Michael Granacki: 18, 37, 41, 101, 133
Nikolas Koenig: 35, 57, 93, 184
Mark Luscombe-Whyte: 68, 186, 196
Bjorg Magnea: 81, 146, 153, 172
Rebecca McAlpin: 33, 82, 125, 171, 181, 183
Jason Schmidt: jacket front, 6, 10, 24, 26, 32, 38, 40, 45, 46, 48, 54, 55, 59, 60, 63, 67, 69, 70, 72, 74, 75, 78, 84, 85, 88, 94, 95, 96, 103, 104, 105, 106, 108, 109, 110, 112, 113, 115, 118, 120, 121, 123 bottom, 126, 127, 130, 134, 138, 139, 140, 142, 144, 145, 149, 152, 155, 159, 165, 173, 178, 180, 187, 190, 191 top, 192, 194, 197, 198, jacket back
Catherine Tighe: 28, 30, 34, 36, 44, 50, 51 top, 52, 56, 58, 62, 66, 73, 77, 79, 80, 83, 86, 87, 91, 92, 97, 102, 114, 116, 117, 123 top, 128, 131, 135, 136, 137, 143, 150, 151, 154, 156, 157, 160, 163 left, 164, 166, 167, 168, 169, 170 top, 175, 176, 177, 182 top